J. DANIELLE

K.I.S.S

Keep It Simple, Sexy

A simple and sexy quick reference

for self-help

Cover and back cover photography and design by Jenae Noonan
Author photo by Maureen Benoit

Victory Publications printed in the United States

For my mom

The fabulous lady in my life who

Taught me without saying a word that sexy is a feeling.

A feeling of empowerment not only through dress,

But by words and how she carries herself.

I love you Mama ♡

Table of Contents

INTRODUCTION... 6

SELF-LOVE...7

ABSOLUTELY, POSITIVELY

THANKFUL... 19

MOVE THAT BODY... 31

FRIENDS... 48

P.M.S.... 60

COZY... 71

SEX... 79

FEARLESS...92

Let's face it... If you know me, you know I've been through a lot. I have experienced multiple marriages, multiple miscarriages, broken relationships, jobs, and death of loved ones which led to so much heartache. In my journey of self-help healing over the past twelve plus years, I have learned a few tips. I like to keep things simple; otherwise, I lose interest quick. Today, society likes to add on layers to get the next level. They have to be the best, have the latest and greatest. But in that, I found that I tend to fall out of whatever it is...things like a new work out, a new phone, a new app, a new route that makes me add on 3 freeways and 20 different streets. I realized, for me to feel accomplished, at ease and happy with myself, I had to keep everything I do as simple as possible. Here, I hope to help you find and remember simple ways to keep you walking in the right direction.

Walking in the direction of your heart, all while feeling sexy.

J. Danielle

CHAPTER 1

SELF LOVE

"Faith in yourself. Believing in yourself. It's about knowing that you were created for a purpose and a reason. So, self-love in that aspect is to live out your life with purpose and meaning." - Joanna Campos

Ok... If you are not living under a rock, I'm sure you have heard someone at some point say that self-love is important. Well, it is. I often give the advice that if you don't take care of yourself first, then what good are you to your partner, your child, your job, and most importantly... yourself?

This is not a selfish love. It is a self-caring love for number one. If your mind goes to the gutter like mine does 85% of the time, then yes, self-love does include "taking care of yourself". You know exactly what I mean (wink, wink, nudge, nudge). But most importantly, self-love is about your heart, mind and entire body. Not just the naughty bits.

"Your relationship with yourself sets the tone for every relationship you have" - Robert Holden

HEART. For anyone who has ever had a broken heart, I hope that you are taking care of this first. If you are over the age of 15 I am pretty sure you have had a broken heart at some point or another. The loss of a first love. A grandparent, a spouse, a friend, a miscarriage, a pet. Loss is different for each one of us. It doesn't matter what it was or who you lost. There was heartache. Healing a broken heart, the right way is so important to your overall health. The right way does not include alcohol, over-eating, sex or online shopping. Although those things feel amazing for a hot second, they do not help you heal. These things can sometimes mask the pain for a short while but prolong healing. If you don't know where to get the help to heal your broken heart, ask around. The help I chose to finally heal all the brokenness inside of me was *The Grief Recovery.* I met with an amazing life coach who led me to do all the healing work myself. She told me that because my heart is inside my body, it means grief/pain/heartache is an inside job. No one on the outside of my body can fix the pain I had. The book is 'The Grief Recovery Handbook' by John W. James and Russell Friedman. They have a team of certified coaches to guide you through the healing process. (For more information on this you can visit https://www.griefrecoverymethod.com)

Before I took the correct steps in healing, I went from one wrong relationship to the next. I would tell myself that it was their fault and not mine. Yes, there were the toxic relationships that I needed to break free from, like an alcoholic partner. But it really does takes two to tango. I had my part in all the pain that came from all these broken relationships too. I would find that I couldn't take it or be in that relationship anymore and break up. I'd take that pain from each relationship and shove it under the imaginary rug. I would work and focus on myself, feel great and move on. But that rug stayed right underneath me the entire time. And when in the next new relationship, something would trigger a painful awkward memory to come above the surface of that rug and mess with me. And I would go through the same vicious cycle and shove that old pain under the rug again. I also had some broken friendships which I had my starring role in. Toxic or not, these friendships had to come to end. Once I took the necessary steps to heal my heart the right way, I felt so free. Free from pain, but also free to make the right decisions for myself going forward. I also had to learn to forgive myself. Forgive myself for mistakes, for past hurts, for hurting others, and for getting into the wrong relationships in the first place. I felt free and light from carrying around all the shit under that rug for so long. I began to listen and trust my heart.

"We are worth way too much to just let our

talents go to waste,"

– Joanna Campos

MIND. Read, learn, listen. There are so many places to get the info needed to take care of yourself. If you like to read, which I hope you do, there are so many self-help books specific for any need or life situation you are going through. There are also many podcasts available for free. Talk to friends or knowledgeable people who may have been around the block once or twice. I'm sure they'd love to share and pass on information that has worked for them. Just ask.

A great more powerful tip and tool is meditation. Find that place where you can go to free your mind of the chatter. This is a great place to relax but also to release anxiety and tension. Meditation does not have to be a full-blown "Eat, Pray, Love" 3-hour session. Once you get the hang of it, meditation can be an easy 5, 10, 15 minutes of clearing your mind. You can add music (I suggest free of words) or sounds like rain and thunderstorms which are my absolute favorite. It's even better if you live in a place where you have frequent rain and thunderstorms unlike me in Southern California. The quickest and easiest way is to find a meditation app to lead you. An app for beginners is usually 15 minutes long and will walk you through the process of clearing your mind. Once you get the hang of meditation, the chatter stops, and you learn to listen to your heart. This is going to sound corny, but this is where you will find yourself. The things in life that should matter will really matter. Although I love prayer for being grateful and asking for the desires of my heart, meditation is not prayer. Meditation is to clear your mind of all the thinking.

Sometimes people say yes, I meditate when I pray. But when you are praying you are also thinking which gets a million thoughts running through your head bringing in the chatter. You are also thinking of other people, and not yourself. Keep prayer time and meditation time separate. Both are very well appreciated by your heart, body and mind.

SEXY TIP: Quick shower meditation

Every time you take a shower, visualize washing away the negatives in your life. Imagine the power of the shower washing and soaping away negative thoughts, anxiety, and stress as they go down the drain. Feel the feelings of freedom, happiness, and joy as you walk out of the shower and dry off. Continue these thoughts throughout your day or evening.

"Continuous improvement is better than

delayed perfection "

- Mark Twain

BODY. Your body is so amazing! Your body heals itself during sleep. Sleep is amazing! When you are sick, you sleep. When you're lacking sleep, you don't function at full capacity. Get as much sleep as you possibly can. And get the sleep needed for your age bracket.

And don't forget to listen to your body. Your body will tell you what you can and cannot do. It will tell you what is good and what is not. If you are tired, rest. If you have a reaction or pain, check-in with yourself and figure out what that is and take care of it. Your body speaks to you daily. Treat your body well. I recently had an issue with my eyelash extensions and my eyebrow gal said my body was rejecting them and to take them off. At first, I didn't listen because I love the look of the extensions. But over time my eyes were too sensitive to handle them and had to be removed. The longer I went without listening to my body and my eyes the longer I suffered from puffy, dry itchy eyelids. That was not pretty.

Get your body moving! Working out makes you feel amazing! Your muscles get toned, burn fat and make you feel and look strong. Exercise is also important for treating and preventing osteoporosis Not only does exercise improve your bone health, it also increases muscle strength, coordination and balance, and it leads to better overall health. I'm realizing that as I get older all of this really does make a big impact on the quality of my life. I can see the effects that working out has on my body. I also love to eat – all kinds of food – so the working out has become the extra push I need so I can partake in all the goodness life has to offer. So, get that body moving!

Walking, dancing, yoga, weights, and my favorite cardio...

SEX! Do it all as much as possible. Your body will thank you

for it.

What are your sexy thoughts about Self-Love?

CHAPTER 2

ABSOLUTELY

POSITIVELY

THANKFUL

"Smiles for sure. Future. Abundance.

Love. Hope. Happiness. "

— Marjorie Darling

THINK POSITIVE. Positive thinking took a little time for me to get. 13+ years I've been training my mind to think of the positive instead of the negative. 13+ years!!! But, in those years I've learned that being grateful goes hand in hand with positive thinking. It really has given my life peace and more meaning. Life started to make more sense once I actually felt the feelings of being grateful. Grateful for my life, my health, my eyes, my hands, my mobility, my family, my friends, my home, my taste buds, my brain, and love I get to share. Thinking positively has made a huge difference in my life when it comes to how I view things – no matter how big or small. The younger me would have thrown a tantrum or gotten moody because something didn't turn out how I planned. Now, if it doesn't go as planned, it was probably for a good reason. My heart and mind see the big picture even though I may not know exactly what the big picture means at that moment. Being grateful and thinking positively has also led me to the things that my heart truly desires. It may not have happened immediately, but it happened. From landing the job, the car, and the house. Now, they may not seem like a big deal to some, but they were big to me. I also receive the little things like unexpected checks in the mail, random gifts, great parking spots and freebies that are least expected.

"Law of attraction, smiling. Happy attitude,

problem solver,

Opportunities, confidence "

– Jazz

THINK. The first thing that led me to positive thinking was reading Rhonda Byrne's 'The Secret'. From that, I learned to train my mind to be grateful and think positively. That led me to so many people and opportunities. Trust me, I am not perfect. It is a daily struggle to not let the negative creep in. Once you get the hang of positive thinking and being grateful you start to see your life shift. Here are some things to think about...

1. THINK OPEN DOORS – instead of thinking you didn't get the job you just interviewed for, think 'This door is not open for me because it may not be the door to the perfect job'. When you train your mind to think like this, you start to see other doors open. Doors that you maybe

had not noticed before. More and more doors will open up. Be open to the opening doors.

2. THINK ME TIME – I used to sit in 1.5 hours of traffic one way each day to work (for just 37 miles). And when people would ask me about my commute they would start to freak out. Well, I loved my job and I loved where I lived. That was my choice to commute to my home and my job. It didn't bother me to drive that every day. I usually responded to people who freaked out about my commute with "That is my ME time. My time in the car to sing out loud, talk too long distant friends, listen to audiobooks and podcasts or just be silent and decompress from the day". People tend to put judgment on your ideas or the way you live, but

you have to remember it is your life. Live it the way that makes sense to you. And try not to make outside opinions or judgments affect you.

3. DON'T SWEAT IT – If you lose something, break something, or forget to do something. Don't sweat it. Things happen for a reason. When you think like this, those things may come back to you in bigger and better ways than you were expecting.

4. CHANGE THE SUBJECT – there are so many negative or judgmental people – everywhere! However, if you choose to be the light in the lives around you, you will see how thinking positively can be contagious. If I am ever around someone speaking negatively or being

judgmental, I let them get whatever it is off their chest. Most times, they are just having a bad day and need to vent about something shitty that happened to them and feel most comfortable with me to do that. However, it's hard not to add fuel to their fire especially if it is someone really close to me. Mama bear tends to come out. I will try to spin the direction of their negative thoughts, with a funny angle, change the subject or point out they're being negative. Usually, this makes the person stop and think, then reflect and separate themselves from the situation at hand.

"Train your mind to see the good in everything. Positivity is a choice. The happiness of your life depends on the quality of your thoughts."

– Marcandange

SEXY NOTE: The Best 6 doctors

SUNSHINE – WATER – REST – AIR – EXERCISE – DIET

FEEL. I don't know about you. But whenever I am outside whether it is overcast, or the sun is shining I feel alive. The brisk air on my face and blowing through my hair gives me so much life. Despite living in Los Angeles with the amount of traffic and crowds I can still find the simple ways the earth is there for me and feel thankful. I can be eating outside in a cool restaurant in Arts District and still hear birds chirping and the rustling of the breeze through the leaves. Knowing full well that when I leave, I may have to pass a drug deal doing down on the corner. Or I can be sitting in traffic on the 405 freeway and notice beautiful flowers blooming. I've seen hummingbirds and dragonflies from my car. Usually, the sight of them makes me pause whatever my thoughts were at that moment, probably cursing traffic, and move to the feelings of being grateful. I even say out loud "Thank you" and immediately, the tension in my body and jaw relax. Now, if I get to be at the beach and hear the waves and feel the salty sea air, I feel so much joy. It's just another way I connect and feel good. I am definitely not a tree hugger or even a big outdoorsy person. I wouldn't choose a tent over a hotel room. I hope you acknowledge those moments in your life and you are thankful for those moments. I hope that you can pause and change from stressed, uptight and negative to peace, calm and joy within seconds. Find the joys in your life and be thankful for them today. These are just some of the simple ways that I connect to the earth which make me feel alive and so thankful for my life.

"I've learned that the more grateful I am, the more I have to be grateful for."

– J. Danielle

SPEAK. As many times as you can say 'Thank you', 'Thanks', 'I am grateful for', say it. Did you just get back change from the cashier? Did someone let you pass in from of them? Wave and mouth the words "thank you". Did someone compliment your new earrings, purse, shoes, or nail polish? Say it and smile. Did someone just hold the door open for you? Did you open the door for someone?

I've done that many times for women and men. Their thank you makes me smile immediately.

"I just like to smile, Smilings my favorite"

— Buddy the Elf

SMILE. Good thoughts make you smile. Good memories make you smile. Be a nice human and smile at strangers who are being courteous. When you smile at another person that person feels it and it feels good. There are neurotransmitters called endorphins that are released when you smile. These are triggered by the movements of the muscles in your face, which is interpreted by your brain, which in turn release these chemicals. Endorphins are responsible for making us feel happy, and they also help lower your stress levels. Yesssss!!!!

What are you absolutely positively thankful for?

CHAPTER 3

MOVE THAT

BODY

"Endorphins. Feeling good. Changing your body.

It's kind of a love-hate relationship" - Mina

PERFECTLY IMPERFECT. I am not the girl with the perfect body. I have stretch marks and cellulite, and I am definitely not skinny. I am average, slightly athletic +10 pounds on a good day. I love to eat, so I work out as much as I can make myself workout. And I cut out where I can. It is a daily struggle. A friend of mine once told me there is a fat girl trapped in my body because I love food so much. Well, I try not to give her everything she wants all the time. Although I have those days or weeks during that time of the month where I can't help myself and just give in to her. Then there are those days when I eat lean and hit the gym 5 times a week. I'm human. I call it balance. What I have learned is that the number that I see on my scale does not define how I feel. I have to feel sexy in my skin no matter what my size or what my scale reads.

Confidence can be the sexiest thing a

woman can ever wear

SEXY TIP: MAGNESIUM (supplement or cream form)

Magnesium activates over 300 enzyme reactions in the

body, translating to thousands of biochemical reactions

happening on a constant daily basis. Magnesium is crucial

to nerve transmission, muscle contraction, blood

coagulation, energy production, nutrient metabolism and

bone and cell formation.

FLAUNT WHAT YOUR MAMA GAVE YOU. I've heard people ask, what is your best asset? For me, it is my legs. Thanks Mama!!!! What is your best asset? Is it your luscious hair, your piercing eyes, your décolletage, your hands, your feet, your waist, your back, or your booty? Whatever it is that you are proud of, flaunt it. Flaunt what your mama gave you! Work it. Play it up. And have fun with it too. The confidence you have will shine through. Remember, don't compare your body with anybody's body. Love your body for all it has done for you so far in life and for what it is capable of doing for you in the future. In turn, your body will love you back.

"Your body hears everything your mind says" – Naomi Judd

SEXY TIP: EVENING PRIMROSE (Oil 1000 mg)

Every woman should be taking this. Great anti-aging supplement. You will see a major improvement in skin tightening and preventing wrinkles. Helps with hormonal acne, PMS, weight control, chronic headaches, menopause, endometriosis, joint pain, diabetes, eczema, MS, infertility, hair, nails, and scalp.

GOAL WEIGHT: SEXY AS FUCK!

MOVE THAT BODY. Find an easy workout that works for you. If you have a gym membership, go. It's that easy. So many people I know pay for a gym membership, yet never go. And if you don't have a gym membership, create an easy workout at home. It doesn't have to be more than 15-30 minutes at least 3 times a week. If you know someone who is an avid gym-goer, ask them for some quick easy work out pointers to get you motivated.

I have a Pinterest board called 'Motivation for Life". It contains easy workouts. I also pin hot bodies to motivate me. Every so often, I will scroll through the workouts and take those ideas to the gym or do them at home. Or I will see a ripped toned woman and get inspired to eat fewer carbs and work out more. I do what I can to keep myself motivated. Find something that works for you and go with it.

If the gym or working out with weights isn't your thing, try yoga. There are so many benefits from yoga for your overall health. Or if you are trying to save money and do not want to pay for a membership, find a simple inexpensive way to move your body. Try to keep it easy so that you don't lose interest or find ways to stop. For me, if I don't go to the gym or if I cancel a membership to save money, I will find walking routes with inclines and beautiful scenery. I usually go with my mom. More times than not we walk towards a goal. A meal. 9 out of 10 times it's a healthy meal.

\

SEXY TIP: Eating an orange before a workout keeps you hydrated, and also prevents your muscles from getting sore.

Try this "LAZY GIRL" workout at home which has 6 fat-burning moves:

1. 20 squat jumps
2. 20 lunges
3. 20 burpees
4. 20 jumping jacks
5. 20 squats
6. 20 crunches

Level I: 1 set

Level II: 2 sets

Level III: 3 sets

If working out or walking is not your thing, be creative. Take the stairs instead of the elevator. Do squats in the kitchen. Do leg lifts while watching your favorite show. Do someone and sweat. Do something to let your body know that you care and plan on keeping it around for a while. Your body may not thank you in the beginning. The soreness and joint pain may keep you from moving your body again, but eventually, you will feel the love from your body. It takes time.

SEXY NOTE: Search the proper way to do any exercise. Especially if you are at home without a trainer to tell you the correct way to do any move. You don't want to chance hurting yourself. Don't let that be the excuse you don't work out again!

SEXY TIP: COLD & HOT SHOWERS

Cold Showers:

Stimulates the immune system, increases alertness, prevents colds, stimulates anti-depression hormones, accelerates your metabolism, frees up the mind, tightens skin, and reduces hair loss.

Try to end your shower in cold water…. Brrrr! But worth it!

Hot Showers:

Relaxes muscles, lowers body tension, alleviates migraines, reduces swelling, reduces anxiety, acts as a nasal decongestant, removes toxins from the skin, opens pores and cleanse the skin. This tends to be easier than a cold shower. However, remember the benefits you get each time you crank up the heat.

SEXY TIP: SEXY WATER TO BOOT WEIGHTLOSS

2L water, 1 medium cucumber, 1 lemon, 10-12 mint leaves. Steep overnight in the fridge. Make and drink every day as a great detox and for clear skin.

"I am imperfect and yet my imperfections, like any great work of art, are what make me a masterpiece. "

— Kelsey Silver

LOVE YOUR BODY. We often forget to love ourselves no matter what size or shape we are in. This goes back to chapter 1 – Self Love and chapter 2 – Positive thinking. Remember, that whatever thought we have about our bodies is exactly what and how we will feel. I am guilty of this almost daily. But I have to stop my negative, self-depleting thoughts and love me just the way I am. Not to love me when I am 10 pounds lighter, when my face thins out, or when I fit into my "skinny jeans". I have to remember to love me for me on a daily basis. Love my stretch marks. Love my thick waist. Love my imperfect ass. And just love me for me. Because of that, I made a list of daily affirmations that I say and believe about myself. When I first created this list, I felt silly about having to say them back to myself. So, the first time I did this, I went in for the full effect and said them in the mirror out loud. And over time I felt love for me. I truly believed what I was saying to me. Now, whenever I have a stressful moment, sad or low point I say them inside my head, out loud in my car, and even when I am facing down on a massage table with acupuncture needles in my back. Sometimes I write on my closet mirror in dry erase markers. Below is a simple list of affirmations for better body confidence. Try these or create your own. Say them to yourself when you wake up and look in the mirror. Or whenever you are having a low point. Remember... whatever you tell yourself, yourself will listen and believe.

AFFIRMATIONS FOR BETTER BODY CONFIDENCE

- I love me

- I am beautiful

- I love my body

- I am grateful for everything my body can do

- I am strong

- I feel peace

- Everything about me is unique and beautiful

- I am fucking AMAZING!

BELIEVE. Believe it or not, your body will respond to you whether it is positive or negative. I truly hope you can start treating your body better. How you feed it will depend on how it will grow. Grow it with good food, positive thoughts and words. Over time you will see your body respond in a positive way. Your relationship with yourself will improve. Your relationships with others may improve too. You may experience confidence, energy, joy and love.

Warning: It will be contagious but oh so sexy!

"Over the years I have learned that what is important in a dress is the woman who is wearing it." – Yves Saint Laurent

SEXY TIP: BENEFITS OF TURMERIC

***Hint: I add turmeric powder to my protein shakes every morning. Just enough to not hate the taste.

- Natural anti-inflammatory
- Natural Antibiotic
- Natural antiseptic
- Natural analgesic
- Speeds up wound healing
- Improves digestion
- Blood purifier
- Strengthens ligaments
- Skin tonic
- Helps coughs
- Improves asthma
- Anti-arthritic
- Slows progression of MS
- Helps prevent gas/bloating
- Helps prevent cancer (breast, prostate, skin, colon, lymphoma, leukemia)
- Prevents progression of Alzheimer's
- Aids in fat metabolism and weight management
- Reduces side effects of chemotherapy

GO EASY ON YOURSELF. If you are just starting to get into the self-care mode of eating better and working out it may seem a little overwhelming to try to remember all these steps either from this book or somewhere else. Go easy on yourself. Try not to push yourself too hard, otherwise, if you are like me you may burn out quickly. So just take on a little bit at a time. Maybe you start with 1 sexy idea or tip to get the hang of it. Do it for a week then add on another one. Remember, it usually takes people doing something seven times before it becomes a habit. I didn't like going to the gym or even working out consistently. I would take a kickboxing class or belly dancing class with a friend and then find a reason to cancel my membership. Or try to do my own at-home workout, but then find a reason to lie on the couch instead. But I signed up for a gym membership and made myself go. The automatic payment part is what really made me go and take it seriously. It was that and the fact that I hit forty. I had to do something. It's been a good three years now that I have been going at least 1-3 times a week. On a busy week, I may only go once, but I go. Because I made it such a big part of my life, I do feel bad if I cannot make it more than once. Now, I say no to a happy hour if I know that it would lessen my days in the gym for the week. I am so proud of myself. I want you to feel proud of yourself too. Whatever it is that you decide to do to show your body love will make you love yourself more. Plus, you will feel sexy. Who doesn't want to feel sexy?

"It is a shame for a woman to grow old without ever seeing the strength and beauty of which her body is capable." – Socrates

What you are plans to get your sexy body moving?

CHAPTER 4

FRIENDS

"Authentic is the word I would use to describe my inner circle... my fierce lady friendships. These friendships are real, they are honest and occasionally they aren't easy. These friendships have stood the test of time, they've been through some things, but they remain, and they aren't going anywhere. At this stage of my life, I'm no longer interested in complicated or drama. So, I stick with my tribe. I would rather have four quarters than a hundred pennies." - Aylcia Carillo

FRIENDS. Whether you have 1 or 10 true friends you can count on, love them. Laugh with them. Create memories with them. And respect them. Treat them just as you would want to be treated. You were put into each other's lives for a reason, or maybe it is only a season? However long it may be, just be the type of friend you would want to have in your life. These friends can also be your family members. These are the people in your life that you call to laugh with, call in an emergency, call for support, or call for no reason but to check in and say hi. They are there for the fun and not so fun times. They become your cheerleaders. But also tell you what you need to hear and not always what you want to hear.

"Love, loyal, fun, family."

— Twinkie T

Don't forget to love on these people as much as you can. Think of the people in your life who you would share special news with. Those are the people who are your true friends, regardless if they are your mother, brother, sister, cousin, a childhood friend, or a new friend. Make them feel special for no special reason at all. Meet for happy hour to keep up with each other's lives. Call when you need a pick me up. Sometimes you just need to hear your friend's reassurance of something you already know the answer to. Stop by for no reason at all and share a bottle of wine. Who cares if the house is a mess? Real friends don't care about silly things like that. Real friends care about you.

"Safety, no judgment, love, laugh, and strength" - Twinkie C

SEXY IDEA: Send a friend an unexpected card in the mail just because... Who doesn't like to get a fun piece of mail that isn't a bill? Maybe you found an old picture back when you both had braces... send it. Who wouldn't get a kick out of that?

"Honesty, understanding, partner-in-crime (in a good way),

Loyalty and laughter are a must."

- Mighty Miss

MEMORIES. Don't let time or distance be the reason you don't see your friends. Take the time to reach out. Life gets busy, but if you reach out to your friends and make the time to see eachother you will be surprised how much the thought and effort are appreciated. Take this time to make new memories with each other. I often hear of friendships where they haven't seen each other in 3-6 months or as long as a year and when they do finally see each other they feel like no time has passed. I have that with my friends too. Time flies, especially as we get older. But all the time that passes is just everyone living their lives. When you get together with your friends you have to catch up for all that lost time. I have a group of best friends from high school. There are 7 of us living in California, and 1 in Colorado. There are a few of us within this group that do get the luxury of seeing each other more than others but not all of us get to be together on a regular basis. Life, children, work and adult responsibilities tend to be the reason. But when we do get together after so much time, we usually spend about an hour going around the table to get caught up on each of our lives. It takes so much time because a few of us become the peanut gallery making funny side commentaries. When we leave each other for the night we are filled up with so much love and excitement. It just adds to the fun bond we have with each other. And it is never a dull moment!

They say nothing lasts forever; dreams change, trends come and go, but friendships never go out of style "

– Carrie Bradshaw

SEXY IDEA: Remember when...?

Pull out a funny story from way back in your memory files... and remind your pals of that funny moment in time. Take them back to that place where you almost

peed your pants from laughing so hard!

"I hope we are friends until we die. And

then I hope we stay ghost friends and walk

through walls and scare the shit out of people."

Unknown

LAUGH. Who doesn't like to laugh? Well, if you don't like to laugh you are not living. Actually, laughing not only eases stress, lowers blood pressure, can boost your immune system, but can help you live longer. Laughing just makes you feel good. And the scientific research on laughter validates the age-old belief that it is at the heart of a healthy life. So, if you aren't going to take my advice from the last chapter to move your body at least you can exercise many of the muscles of your body as you laugh in addition to releasing endorphins. Spending time with your friends laughing at something or nothing at all is the best medicine anyone can ask for. Recently, funny memes have been the center for many of the laughs I share with my friends. We can easily spend a good 30 minutes laughing about it or move on to the next belly laugh within 3 seconds. Laughter really is the best medicine. So next time you hear a good joke, see something funny, or do something yourself that deserves a good laugh share it with your friends. Startup a group chat to share what you just experienced. Send that picture of your kid's haircut after they got a hold of the scissors. Then laugh about it together.

"Loyalty, compassion, laughs"

– Rebecca Lynn Chin

SEXY TIP: MAKE PLANS WITH YOUR FRIENDS... And stick to them.

PLAN. Now that we are all grown up and have such busy lives, we hardly see each other. We hardly get to see each other. But, when we do, we have a blast, and usually, leave each other with sore bellies and sore throats from laughing and talking so much. We have kept 2 annual parties that we do not miss for anything. We have a summer party and a winter party. Just us girls. No husbands, boyfriends, or children. We look forward to these events every year. Yes, there are the happy hours or dinners that we plan in between these main events, but usually, one or two people cannot make it. The build-up to the big events are great. We talk about it and get so excited months before we go. Sometimes we have themes, and other times it is all about food & drinks and just getting away to be with each other. We have so much fun and look forward to these events each year. They have become major traditions in our lives. Everyone around us knows we will not cancel or miss out.

"Trustworthy, laughter, loyal."

– Tove Sanz

SEXY CELEBRATIONS: Don't forget to celebrate everything, anything, and nothing at all with your friends. Engagements, divorces, new jobs, babies, puppies, weight loss, new car, new home, new boyfriend/girlfriends. Anything to clink glasses and spend time with friends is worth every minute. Make your circle of friends feel special

for no special reason at all.

What are some ideas to make your sexy friends smile?

CHAPTER 5

P.M.S.

"DRAMA. It's like your body is trying to teach you something but your mind gets stuck in the drama, so you can't really pay attention to what's real. It's some kind of woman fog." - Vanessa

LITERALLY, PMS'ING AS I TYPE THIS CHAPTER! Seriously, I couldn't have picked a more appropriate time to write this chapter than today. Two days ago, I woke up angry. My hair was dirty. My nails looked like I single-handedly tore down a building. My lashes were falling off and I didn't have an appointment for another week. I was so bloated my baggie jeans were tight. My tits were sore. I looked and felt like crap. Ugh! And I really had to refrain from raging at my co-workers. Poor them. No... POOR ME!!! Luckily, after hours of running around taking care of shit at work and staying away from stupid people I got to end the day with an orgasm all by myself. Tension relieved. I almost passed out. But today I ate 2 lunches because I was really hungry but also because I couldn't choose. My uterus is throbbing. I'm tired. My body hurts all over. My head hurts. I'm grumpy. I'm crying over a car commercial. No one is paying attention to me. I'm short-fused. And I have a huge zit on my cheek. And I'm still hungry. I know that once my period starts, I will be ok... But right now, I think I've been possessed. HELP! Send snacks!

"P.M.S. = time to eat whatever I want and if you tell me I'll get fat I'll eat you too"

—Denshai

HORMOTIONAL. I love it when I get to be home and stay in bed during these hormotional times. I love being in my sweats, no make-up, braless, eating, watching Hallmark movies and crying over high school sweethearts falling back in love, and my all-time favorite - a proposal! Waaaaa!!! But, sometimes depending on the month and the moon my P.M.S. doesn't fall on a weekend. I have to be at work and function like a normal human being, which is really hard to do.

"P.M.S. = Possible, Mental, Snap...

Bitches beware "

– Shana "Maker of Magic" Cross

SEXY NOTE: Did you know that a 20-second hug releases the bonding hormone and neurotransmitter oxytocin, which is nature's antidepressant and anti-anxiety.

Make someone hug you today, dammit!

TAKE CARE. I have to remind myself that this is the time for me to take care of me. Indulge in the things that make me happy - within reason. Take long baths. Curl up on the couch or in bed and binge watch a series. Eat a Cinnabon or an entire chocolate Bundt cake. Or just talk about it for 2 weeks which is usually what I do. Whatever makes me happy. I have to remember to always check in with myself. You should know by now how you are going to feel during this time of the month. Be gentle with yourself. I'm realizing that every month is going to be different. For me, lately, if I am having a really emotional time, it just means my period is going to be short and sweet. Then, the very next month, my emotions are easy breezy, but my uterus hates me, and I feel like I am going to bleed to death. Every month is different. I just need to remember to take care of me no matter what.

"Ugh... Oh God! Draining the life out of me."

— Tracey

LOVE YOUR BODY. I would love to skip the gym this week, but this is the time that my body needs it the most. I have to push myself to go because I would rather crawl into bed after work. Once I go, I end up feeling so much better. Yoga is the best during PMS. Especially if the instructor is calm and talks me through being gentle on myself and my practice. My body also needs sleep. I try to get as much sleep as possible. Most nights during this time, I literally just pass out. The hard part is loving myself through this time. I get mad that my clothes are tighter, and my skin breaks out. Why does my body need to treat me like this? I shouldn't be punished for not getting pregnant! But no, it doesn't work like that. We have to remember that our bodies are miraculous vessels here to do amazing things in life. Let's remember to be kind to our beautiful bodies – A L W A Y S!

"Sorry I OVARY-acted"

SEXY TIPS: Happy Pills – Alternative therapies for PMS

- Evening Primrose
- Omega 3
- Magnesium
- Vitamin D
- Calcium
- Zinc
- Selenium
- Vitamin B6
- Folic Acid
- Chasteberry
- Valerian root
- Tryptophan
- Ginkgo Biloba
- St. John's Wort
- Passion Flower

SEXY TIP: Once a week for 20 minutes, sit in a hot bath that contains a handful of Epsom salts, 10 drops of lavender essential oil, and a half cup of baking soda. This combo draws out toxins, lowers stress-related hormones, and balances your pH levels.

"Yes, I'm being a bitch and I couldn't give two F*CKS." - E.B.R

MEN. They just don't understand. They really don't. I wish they did. I know they too have PMS, but there is no comparison. It isn't something that is easily tracked, and it doesn't happen every 28 days. For me to be in a happy normal state-of-mind one day and then 5 days prior to starting my period I become possessed is ridiculous. Seriously! I feel like someone evil has entered my body and wants to ruin every relationship around me. Now, don't get me wrong. I once had a boyfriend who knew my cycle. I would come home to a glass of wine, flowers, and dinner made. He either knew I would be in a rage and didn't want to cross me, or he just knew the emotional state I was going to be in and wanted to help alleviate my stresses and make me feel better. God bless that man wherever he may be. But here I am without that man for other reasons beyond my control. A lot of men think that it is something that can be controlled. I wish it was that simple. But when you are being possessed, it is really out of your control. Honestly, sex works for me. Now, that is simple. Personally, I am a little hornier during PMS week. I know it is different for everyone. But at least I know what works for me. Find out what it is that works for you and let your partner know. Or give a heads up that PMS is upon you. A fair warning should work. Like shark week, you know it's coming, so just be prepared for it.

"Why are you so fucking annoying? Why am I crying?" - Suzette

How will you take care of yourself during your P.M.S?

_____

_____

_____

_____

_____

_____

_____

_____

_____

_____

CHAPTER 6

COZY

"The older I get, the more I realize how much I love being home."

- J. Danielle

JUST CHILL. I love that this chapter follows PMS….
Whether I am menstruating or just want to chill from a
long week, I love being cozy at home, especially during the
colder months. In my twenties, I wanted to be anywhere
but home. I needed to be out and be seen with all the hair
and all the make-up and all the skin showing. But now that
I am not in my twenties anymore, I appreciate being
home. The feeling of my comfortable stretchy pants, no
bra, slippers (or "chanclas" as I grew up calling them), hair
up on top of my head, my bed and my TV makes me so
happy. I'm at the point now in life that if I have a free
weekend, I don't make plans and don't let anyone know
that I don't have plans. Shhh! I just love it.

"I love my bed. We're perfect for each other. But for some reason, my alarm clock doesn't want us to be together. That jealous whore!"

– Anonymous

NAP. Adults don't nap enough. Or maybe it is just me. I feel like I need to be sick to take a nap. Or just be completely hungover which is terrible, I know. Maybe it is the fear of missing out on the sunlight, or maybe not, because I tend to stay up late too. But when it is time to crash, I crash hard. I know that sleep is so good for me. In chapter one, I mention that your body heals itself during sleep. It is so true…. Remember to take advantage of being in your cozies at home and nap. It's not just for night time.

"Fuzzy blanket. My dog. I guess my fiancé can be there too. And sweats."

— Tracey

HOME. Call me crazy, but I look forward to doing my laundry when I am home, separating of the colors, then separating clothes from the linens. It's so therapeutic to me. So, when I am home, I do all the laundry and binge watch anything. And sometimes, when the mood strikes, I purge my closet in between loads. I put my diffuser on with sensual oils and light candles throughout my house. My favorite music may be playing in the background. I'm totally in my home-girl mode. I purge my closet about every three months and call my sisters or girlfriends over to go through my things. I love it. It feels amazing. Find that something that you enjoy doing when you are home and relish in it. Be thankful for those days that you aren't hectically running around trying to check off your to-do lists. Light the special candles or put on an air diffuser with yummy scents to make you feel cozy.

SEXY SMELLS: Aromatherapy in the home is fantastic for any mood. Find an oil diffuser and just add water and oils to boost your mood. Lavender for relaxation at night. Sweet orange as an energy booster in the morning. Sandalwood and Patchouli for setting the mood, any time of the day!!! I also have a diffuser for my office. Sweet orange to keep the energy going. And eucalyptus during the cold months to kill bacteria. And, as always, please read instructions of the diffuser you purchase and the oils you chose to use. Breathe in and enjoy.

"Your home should tell the story of who you are and be a collection of what you love."

— Nate Berkus

CUDDLE. If you are in a relationship, enjoy those moments you are both home and feel sexy together. Cuddle on the couch or in bed. Give each other massages, or just lay in bed all day — naked. Cuddling also releases oxytocin and endorphins. Medical professionals say this can give you a sense of well-being and make you feel like you had a good work out or ate a piece of chocolate. Cuddling also releases dopamine, which increases sexual desire. And we all know what sexual desire leads to.... An orgasm... or two. So, the next time you and your partner are home together being cozy, don't forget to cuddle. And don't forget to cuddle with your furbabies if you have them. Furbabies love when you are home and get to be cozy with you.

"I like all my goodies with me (drinks, snacks... etc.), wearing my comfy clothes, feeling safe, and snuggling."

- Jazz

ENJOY. Surround yourself with your favorite things and enjoy the coziness of your home... Candles, sweats, music, chocolate, tea, a cocktail. Do whatever it is that makes you feel warm and fuzzy and sit back and enjoy. Or maybe blasting music and dancing around your kitchen is something you enjoy doing. Take the time to enjoy being home. Alone or with the ones you love.

What makes you feel cozy?

CHAPTER 7

S E X

"Passion. Love. Energy. Explosive energy.

Freedom. Ability to be a freak."

- Daniel

SEX IS SO GOOD. To have and experience. A lot of it. Quickie or not, it is great. I hope every mature adult is enjoying sex in a responsible way as much as possible. The sense you get when you are with your partner. You look at each other and immediately get turned on. You know you are both going to end up sweaty and out of breath. It is so intoxicating. Even the mundane sex at the end of the night when you are tired can end with an orgasm if you really want it to. You know the kind. Your partner is ready to go, and you really just want to be left alone. Use that time to get yours. It doesn't just have to be about your partner's needs. You have needs too. You may not realize how much good an orgasm can do for you as you drift off to sleep. No need for Ambien or melatonin here. There is scientifically backed evidence that shows having an orgasm helps you sleep better. The brain releases beneficial hormones during and after sex which includes endorphins, serotonin and oxytocin just to name a few. So, if you're thinking about taking a hard pass on sex, don't. Just do it. Even if it is just for the plain and simple reason of a good night's sleep.

"Feels good. Fun. Necessary. Gets better with age, with how long you are with your partner and with how confident you are with yourself."

– Tracey

SEXY NOTE: People who have sex have higher levels of what defends your body against germs, viruses, and other intruders. Get it on and stay healthy!

There is a study that found participants who had intercourse were better able to handle stress in many situations (including public speaking) than those who had not had intercourse. And we all know that sex releases brain endorphins, which automatically lifts your mood and helps relieve stress and reduce inflammation in the body. Endorphins are the body's natural painkillers. This is why I truly believe that sex or having an orgasm helps with headaches and body aches. Or stomach aches. And premenstrual cramps. It's funny to me that people use the "I have a headache" excuse to get out of having sex. Don't get me wrong, I have used it before, but that was a blatant lie to get out of sex with a partner that didn't do it for me. That was my cue to get out of that relationship. At that time, I didn't realize all the benefits that an orgasm would have on me. But now I do. Next time you have a headache try having an orgasm or two and see how much better you feel after.

Sometimes you just need a hug, in the vagina, with a penis.

Do you ever feel like sex is a chore or like it is more for your partner than for you? For all of you that feel this way... Stop! It may just be a dry spell. Whatever it is stop over thinking and make it for you and about you. Forget how tired you are and do it for all the amazing benefits. Do it because it feels good. Do it because you can. Do it because you want to.

"Mija, once you start having sex your skin will clear up."

- Grandma Cece (circa, 1992)

SKIN. My grandmother said that to me when I was a teenager. Believe it or not, I was shocked when that came out of her mouth. I think most of my family reading this today will be shocked too. I am not sure that she was right about that because in my 40's I am still breaking out. Even with sex on a regular basis. But it sure made me listen. She was definitely on to something. I firmly believe that. Take a look at some of the benefits that sex has on your body.

- Boosts your immune system = fewer sick days = more days for real vacations
- Improve's women's bladder control
- Lowers blood pressure
- Lowers heart attack risk
- Can reduce pain sensation and increase your pain threshold
- May reduce prostate cancer
- May help your memory
- Lowers stress, anxiety and depression by releasing good for your hormones
- Good sex improves sleep (only the good kind)
- Counts as exercise

Cuddle often. Kiss a lot. Be naughty. Have a

lot of sex.

Love deeply. Be happy.

KISS. I hope you still kiss your partner. Long make-out sessions, during sex, not during sex. I once had a boyfriend that asked, "Why don't we make out?" I realized at that moment that I didn't want to make out with him because of him not because I didn't like kissing. It was just way too messy and slimy. My mouth was assaulted by his tongue darting in and out. And the spark and chemistry were missing. That was my cue to go! But if you have that person in your life who you love to kiss any time of the day, even in the morning prior to brushing teeth. Kiss them! Those lingering hot passionate kisses while passing each other in the hallway. Even the simple ones when you walk through the door at the end of the day. I love them all.

SEXY KISSING BENEFITS:

- *Helps reduce blood pressure*

- *Relieves cramps and headaches*

- *Fights cavities*

- *Happy hormones are elevated*

- *Burns about 6.4 calories a minute*

- *Boosts self-esteem*

- *Is a barometer for sexual compatibility*

"Find that person that can make you laugh in public and scream in bed."

ENJOY. It is so important that you enjoy having sex with your partner. You think of your partner and immediately get turned on. Sometimes we get into relationships or marriages where the sex starts to become less and less. This may be because of lulls in your relationship, outside stresses or children. Try to bring it back to that time when you couldn't keep your hands off of each other. Talk about your fantasies and make them come true together. Send a naughty text before you both get from work. The buildup is exciting, especially if you are talking about it out in public in a very private way. You can't wait to get each other naked. Every touch. Every moan. Every smell. Enjoy the foreplay. Enjoy the buildup.

THEN DO IT. Do it in the morning. Do it in the car. Do it in a plane. Do it in the kitchen. Do it on your patio. Do it in the stairwell. Do it in the closet. Do it on the floor. Do it leaning over the couch. Do it in the shower. Do it with all the windows open. Do it when you're hungover. Do it in front of a mirror. Do it fast. Do it slow. Do it in 30 minutes. Do it in 3 minutes. And no matter how you do it, enjoy doing it. And then when you are finished... Love the glow. Love the messy hair. Love the fast heartbeats. Love the smile on your face and all the tingles in your body. Wherever and however you decide to do it, take a deep breath and just enjoy it. Get out of your bedroom and do it. And if budget permits, get a hotel room. No need to get out of town. Get a room in your neighborhood for the change of scenery or just to spice things up. Sometimes changing the scenery allows inhibitions to fly out the window. I know it does for me.

DILDO: The original selfie-stick

Hopefully, you get it on a regular basis with your partner. And if not, you need a new partner. Or, your B.O.B. (Battery Operated Boyfriend) should fill in when necessary. Just be sure you are being safe. Make sure the both of you are healthy and not spreading any nasty STD's around. Always be safe and take care of your body. And if you are playing with your B.O.B alone or with your partner, please be careful. No one needs a "sex sent me to the ER" episode in their life.

YOU. For those of you who are not in a long-term committed relationship and are not sleeping around... You should have your favorite vibrator and trusty hand to do the job. YOU are in total control and can be selfish. Who cares if you didn't shave your legs? YOU don't even need to have dinner and drinks first. YOU can just go for it. Have 1orgasm. Have 2. And then have a 3rd. Who cares? YOU. Only YOU.

SHOP. If you don't have a vibrator, grab a friend and hit up your local adult store. Ask the salespeople for their top picks. Usually, if the store is not creepy, they have very professional educated staff. They will ask you what it is that you are looking for. From there they will guide you to purchase the right one for you. My girlfriend and I go and have a great time. And if all that sounds like something out of your comfort zone, go online. There are plenty of websites that have a great selection and will arrive at your door completely discreet.

Mmm... Thoughts and ideas to keep it sexy:

_____

_____

_____

_____

_____

_____

_____

_____

CHAPTER 8

FEARLESS

"Brave, bold, self-assured, gutsy,

heroic, adventurous."

– Jen B

BRAVE. It has taken a long time for me to feel fearless, yet alone be fearless. But here I am writing a book. For years, I said I wanted to write a book. And for years, I did nothing. Opportunities would come, and I would step back and hide. I hid behind relationships, my job, and my own fear. Fear would take over and make me immobile. But one day, little by little I looked fear in the face and told that bitch who I am. I am the woman with dreams. I am the woman with passion. I am the woman with love in my heart. I am the woman who actually does things that I say I am going to do. I may not complete them all on time, but at least I start them.

"Love, Strength, Empowered, Superwoman, Strong, Badass."

– Vivi Angelica Veloso

STRENGTH. Being fearless can mean so many things to each one of us. Rollercoaster's, sky-diving, having a child, taking a new job, public speaking, surgery, meeting new people, fighting for a cause and helping a stranger are some examples of what some might view as fearless. But at the core, it seems to be the same thing. It's doing the things that get you out of your comfort zone. Not really giving a fuck what other people think. Only what you think, and how you feel is what matters the most. Once you do that, whatever it is, you feel empowered and liberated. For me, being fearless changed the way I look at life. It's not that I am fearless in everything that I do. I still have the things in life that scare me. But, little by little I challenge myself to do them. For me, the big one has been saying "no". I am such a "yes" girl, a people pleaser, but I realized that just made me mad for doing shit for others and not having enough time to take care of my personal shit. But now, I pick and choose what I say "yes" to and saying "no" to things that don't serve me or my life. I feel bad saying "no". But after I say it, I feel better about myself. I don't tend to spread myself too thin leaving very little for me anymore. This goes back to Chapter 1 – Self-love. I've come full circle.

"Courage, flow, faith, trust."

– Kim Somers Egelsee

TRUST. Don't be afraid to do the things that will set your heart on fire. Don't be afraid to go after your dreams, your goals, and your passions. Whatever they are – do them. Go after them. Achieve them. We are the youngest we will ever be today. Don't let life pass you by. You don't want to ever think 'I should have done this or that'. Do it. If anything, do it for the stories to pass on to your children.

Do it for the WOW factor. Or do it because you will kick yourself if you didn't. Trust in yourself to do and become whatever you want. We only have this life on earth. Squash fear and tell that motherfucker who's in charge. I AM! YOU ARE! WE ARE!

"Warrior. Goddess."- Tangee

SEXY NOTE: The phrase "do not be afraid" is written in the bible 365 times. That's a daily reminder from God to live every day being FEARLESS.

"Strong, courageous, walking through the storm, head held high."

- Kathleen Kenneally

COURAGEOUS. Every New Year, we give ourselves a list of resolutions that usually don't get accomplished. This year, whether it is the beginning, middle or end of the year, give yourself just one fearless mission to complete. I challenge you! Do that for yourself. Is it adrenaline? Is it being alone? Giving up sugar? How about dating after a divorce? They're all scary. But imagine how you will feel once you do it? Empowered is how you will feel. Put yourself out there and do it.

"Honest, self-confident, worthy,

risk-taker, faith. "

– Claudia

FAITH. Have the faith in yourself to take care of you the way you know you deserve. Have faith in yourself to make the right decisions for yourself. Have faith in making mistakes. We have to remember, that we are not perfect. We make mistakes. And mistakes help mold us to be better people. Just remember to learn from those mistakes and have faith in yourself to make the right choice next time.

"Confident, nothing will stop you"

– Melody

SEXY TIP: 6 Things that can change your life in one year

1. Stop complaining and be grateful for who you are and what you have right now.

2. Be OK to be alone.

3. Say goodbye to negative people and hello to positive people.

4. Pick one goal and commit to it.

5. Workout at least 3-5 times a week for 15 minutes.

6. Fail. Learn from every mistake you make and keep moving forward.

"Think like a queen. A queen is not afraid to fail. Failure is another stepping stone to greatness."
– Oprah

What will you do to be FEARLESS?

_____

_____

_____

_____

_____

_____

_____

_____

_____

_____